Grandfather's Journal

Grandfather's Journal

MEMORIES AND KEEPSAKES FOR MY GRANDCHILD

Laura M. Westdale

Bluestreak
BOOKS

*Bluestreak*

an imprint of Weldon Owen International
1150 Brickyard Cove Road
Richmond, CA 94801

© 2018 Weldon Owen

Library of Congress Cataloging in Publication data is available.

ISBN-13: 978-1-68188-362-5

First printed in 2018
2024 2023 2022 2021 2020
12 11 10

Printed in China

ILLUSTRATION CREDITS:

©iStockPhoto/Para-Graph: cover, pocket; ©shutterstock/PinkPueblo: 1, 3; ©iStockPhoto/filo: 2, 15 bottom; ©shutterstock/Reljic Aleksandra: 5; ©iStockPhoto/Oksancia: 6–7; ©iStockPhoto/aleksandarvelasevic: 7 (dingbat); ©iStockPhoto/eduardrobert: 8–9; ©iStockPhoto/dzubanovska: 10–11, 26–27, 40–41, 54–55, 74–75; ©iStockPhoto/mxtama: cover (dingbat), 12, 13, 28, 29, 30, 31, 33, 43, 62, 63, 67, 71, pocket (bird); ©iStockPhoto/AnnaFrajtova: 14, 15 top, 44, 45, 84, 85; ©iStockPhoto/Pleasureofart: 16; ©iStockPhoto/bluebearry: 17, 60, 61; ©iStockPhoto/lublubachka: 18, 19; ©iStockPhoto/CSA-Archive: 20, 21, 90, 91; ©iStockPhoto/PinkPueblo: 22, 23, 68, 69, 80, 81; ©iStockPhoto/Bigmouse108: 24, 25 top; ©iStockPhoto/Diane Labombarbe: 25 bottom; ©shutterstock/MuchMania: 34, 35; ©shutterstock/Mushakesa: 36, 37, 46, 47 top, 88, 89 top; ©iStockPhoto/cafillu: 38, 39; ©shutterstock/Macrovector: 47 bottom, 89 bottom; ©shutterstock/Aleutie: 49; ©shutterstock/yoolarts: 50 top; ©shutterstock/Ivan Baranov: 50 bottom; ©shutterstock/NorSob: 51; ©shutterstock/LanaN: 52, 53, 94, 95; ©shutterstock/Lubenica: 56; ©shutterstock/xenia_ok: 57; ©iStockPhoto/alecsia: 58, 59; ©iStockPhoto/mashuk: 64, 65, 86, 87 top; ©shutterstock/stockshoppe: 72; ©shutterstock/chelovector: 73; ©iStockPhoto/kimikodate: 76, 77; ©shutterstock/Olga Milagros: 78, 79; ©iStockPhoto/zacky24: 82–83; ©iStockPhoto/Angel_1978: 87 bottom; ©shutterstock/Oksana Alekseeva: 92, 93; ©iStockPhoto/A-Digit: 96

Contents

Introduction

A Private Note to Grandkids from the Publisher

The love we give away is the only love we keep.

—ELBERT HUBBARD

We're going to print this note really small, so your granddad can't read it. It's private, only for you.

You already know that grown-ups were kids once, but have you ever really thought about what your grandfather was like when he was your age? What did he look like when he started school? What did he like to do when he was a teenager? How did he meet your grandmother? Where was he when your mom or dad was born? What was the thing your parent did that made him the proudest…or the maddest, and why?

This journal is his place to tell you the things about himself and your family history that you will want to know one day, even if you don't realize it yet.

And as you grow up, you will treasure this special keepsake, in which your grandfather has shared his stories, dreams, and wisdom—just for you! So even if it seems like a weird gift now, hold on to it, talk to your grandfather about it, ask him to tell you more stories and find pictures you can keep in it, and one day you will be very happy that you did!

My Family Tree

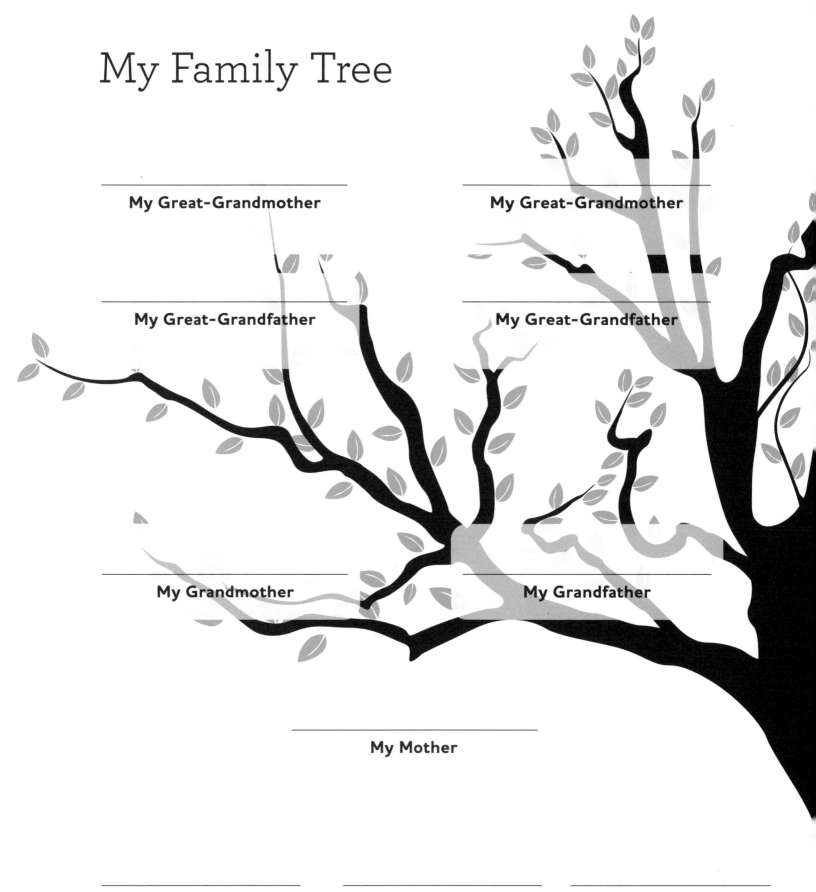

My Great-Grandmother

My Great-Grandmother

My Great-Grandfather

My Great-Grandfather

My Grandmother

My Grandfather

My Mother

Me

My Sibling

My Sibling

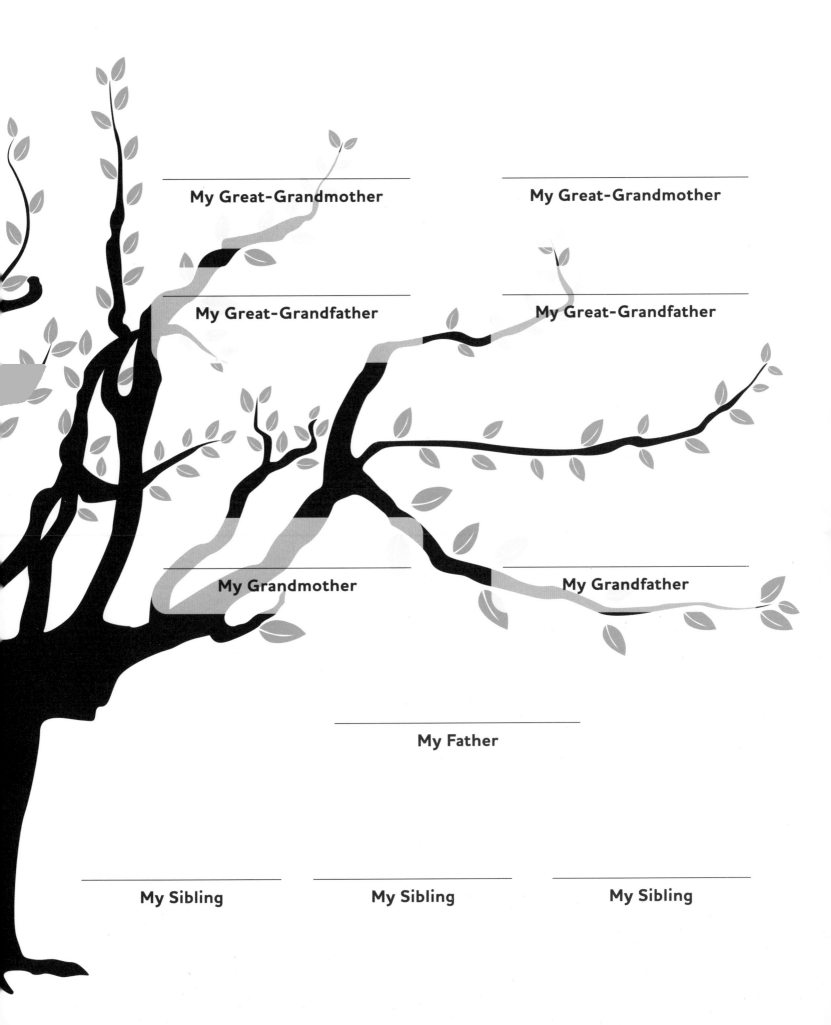

My Great-Grandmother

My Great-Grandmother

My Great-Grandfather

My Great-Grandfather

My Grandmother

My Grandfather

My Father

My Sibling

My Sibling

My Sibling

CHAPTER ONE

About Me and My Family

When I Was Born

To be yourself in a world that is constantly trying to
make you something else is the greatest accomplishment.

—RALPH WALDO EMERSON

I was born in

which is near

My family's address was

My birthday is

My parents named me (full name)

They chose my name because

My nickname(s):

THE OTHER MEMBERS OF MY FAMILY

Brothers (dates of birth):

Sisters (dates of birth):

About My Parents

A wise parent humors the desire for independent action, so as
to become the friend and advisor when his absolute rule shall cease.

—ELIZABETH GASKELL, from *North and South*

My parents (your great-grandparents!) were named

and

My mother was born in

My father was born in

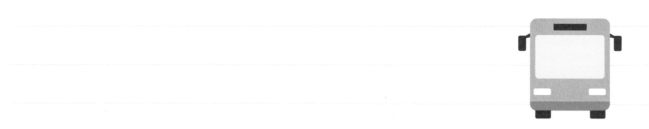

14

How my parents met:

When and where they married:

My parents earned their living by

Some things I remember about my mother:

Some things I remember about my father:

My mother's interests:

My father's interests:

My siblings' interests:

Where we lived:

Qualities I got from my mother:

Qualities I got from my father:

Something I would like you to know about my mother:

Something I would like you to know about my father:

The stories we always told about growing up in our family:

Memories and moments I want to share about my family when I was growing up:

About My Grandparents
(Your Great-greats!)

Few parents nowadays pay any regard to what their children say
to them. The old-fashioned respect for the young is fast dying out.

—OSCAR WILDE, *from The Importance of Being Earnest*

My mother's parents were named _____

_____

_____

They lived in _____

_____

_____

Their other children—my aunts and uncles—were named (include birthdates)

_____

_____

_____

_____

They made their living by _____

_____

The things I most remember about them are _____

_____

_____

_____

My father's parents were named _____

_____

_____

_____

They lived in _____

_____

Their other children—my aunts and uncles—were named (include birthdates) _____

_____

_____

_____

They made their living by _____

_____

_____

The things I most remember about them are _____

_____

_____

About Our Family's Heritage

Every generation revolts against its
fathers and makes friends with its grandfathers.

—LEWIS MUMFORD, from *The Brown Decades*

My family's nationality is

Our ethnic background is

My relatives came from these places:

The origins of our family name are

My favorite relative growing up was

because

Some traditions that we observed from our ethnic heritage were

We also followed these religious traditions:

I remember hearing these stories about our family's history:

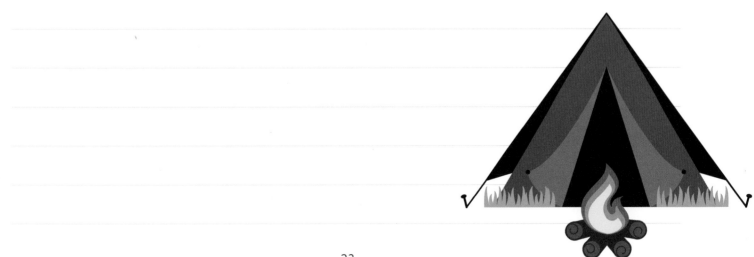

Food Traditions

After a good dinner one can forgive anybody,
even one's own relations.

—OSCAR WILDE, from *The Importance of Being Earnest*

Some of the foods my family liked to eat were _____

_____

_____

_____

Traditional family dishes that we ate were _____

_____

_____

Something I remember well about family meals when I was growing up: _____

_____

_____

Our family had these rules/habits about dinnertime: _____

_____

_____

_____

_____

_____

My favorite foods as a child were _____

_____

_____

_____

A food I really did not like was _____

_____

_____

Some dishes we ate on special occasions were _____

_____

_____

_____

_____

CHAPTER TWO

About Me Growing Up

About My Home

*The happiest moments of my life have been the few
which I have passed at home in the bosom of my family.*

—THOMAS JEFFERSON

Where I lived when I was a young boy:

What I remember about my family's home:

My room was

I would describe our neighborhood (include the name if you can) as

We had a pet(s) named

My best pal(s) were

When I played with my siblings or friends, we

Favorite games:

Favorite places:

If I got in trouble, my parents would

A memory I want to share with you from when I was a little boy:

My Elementary Years

To repeat what others have said, requires education;
to challenge it, requires brains.

—MARY PETTIBONE POOLE

My elementary school was called

My favorite teacher was

My favorite subjects in school were

I got to school by

After school, most days I would

A memory I have from elementary school:

My Middle School Years

The...goal of education is to form minds which can be critical,
can verify, and not accept everything they are offered.

—JEAN PIAGET

My middle school was called

My favorite teacher was

My favorite subjects in school were

I got to school by

The things I liked to do after school were

Some of my best friends from middle school were

My extracurricular activities and hobbies:

A memory I have from middle school:

My High School

An education isn't how much you have committed to memory, or even how much you know. It's being able to differentiate between what you do know and what you don't. It's knowing where to go to find out what you need to know; and it's knowing how to use the information you get.

—MARY PETTIBONE POOLE

I went to high school at

My favorite teacher was

My favorite subjects in school were

I got to school by

The things I liked to do after school were

Some of my best friends from high school were

My extracurricular activities and hobbies included

When I Was a Teen

Youth is a wonderful thing. What a crime to waste it on children.

—GEORGE BERNARD SHAW

I was the kind of guy who always _____

_____

_____

I was the kind of guy who sometimes _____

_____

_____

I was the kind of guy who never _____

_____

_____

My favorite kind of music was _____

_____

_____

I used to listen to it while I was _____

_____

_____

I played (or liked) this instrument: _____

_____

How we listened to music when I was a teen: _____

_____

_____

Songs that meant a lot to me when I was a teenager: _____

_____

_____

Musicians I admired included _____

_____

_____

_____

Songs or musicians I would like to share with you (and why): _____

_____

_____

_____

_____

_____

A story about listening to music that I want to share with you:

These are a few of my favorite books and authors from when I was young:

A story or book that meant a lot to me when I was a kid was

Some books that I hope you will read and enjoy one day:

These are a few of my favorite TV shows and movies from when I was young: _____

_____

_____

_____

One show or movie that meant a lot to me when I was a kid was _____

_____

A movie or show that I hope we will watch together is _____

_____

I was athletic/not so much. _____

I liked to be outdoors/indoors. _____ ,

In my spare time, I liked to _____

_____

_____

When I was a teenager, most kids would wear _____

_____

_____

_____

_____

My signature outfit or look was _____

_____

I wore my hair _____

_____

My best friend(s) _____

_____

What we liked to do: _____

_____

_____

_____

_____

My social life was _____

_____

_____

Someone who had a big influence on me was _____

_____

because _____

_____

_____

During the summers, we used to

Overall, I would describe my teenage years as

A memory from my teen years that I want to share with you:

Something I learned as a teenager that I think you might like to know:

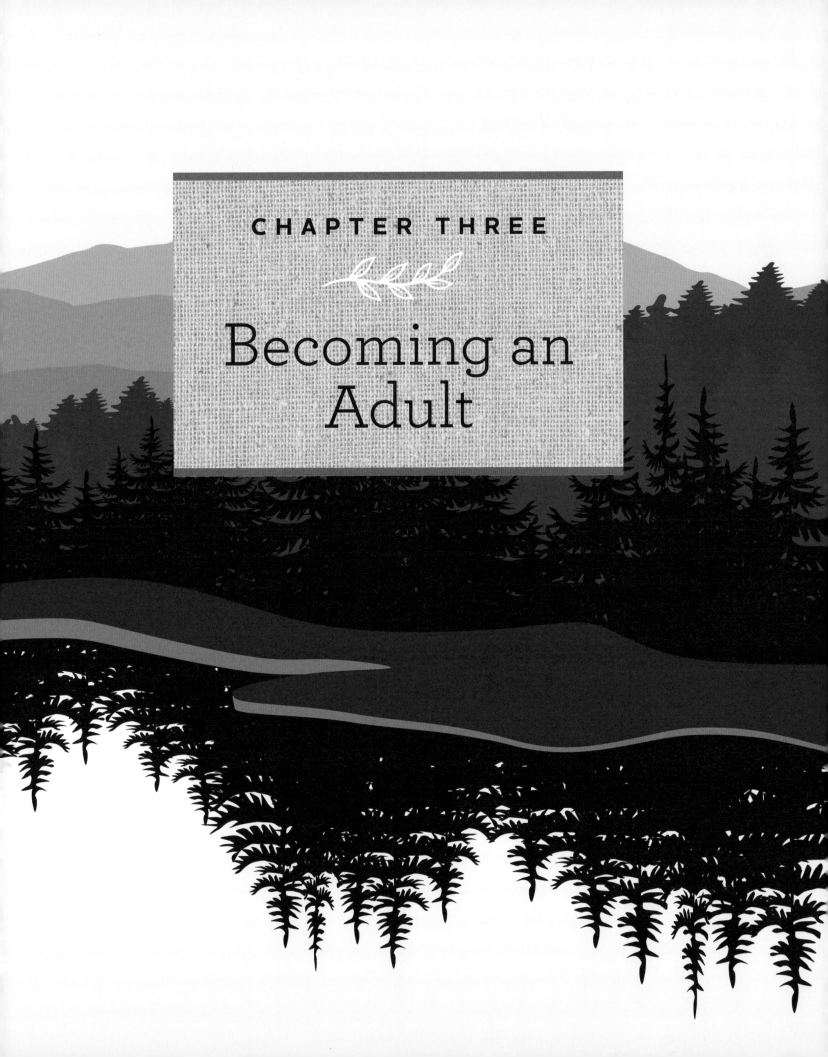

CHAPTER THREE

Becoming an Adult

On My Own

Home is where one starts from. As we grow older the
world becomes stranger, the pattern more complicated . . .

—T. S. ELIOT, from *Four Quartets*

After high school, the first thing I did was

Then I (continued with school, got a job, joined the military . . .)

I lived (where, with whom . . .)

I studied/learned

What was important to me back then was

My social life was

Some of my best memories from those years are

My dreams and goals in those years included

Something I learned in my early twenties that I want to share with you:

My Early Career

Hard work never hurt anyone.

—MODERN PROVERB

The first (or most interesting) real job I had was _____

_____

_____

It entailed _____

_____

_____

What I liked about it: _____

_____

_____

What I didn't like about it: _____

_____

_____

What I learned from my first job that I want to share with you:

The next step in my career was

The things I enjoyed most during that time were

And the things I didn't like:

My dreams at that time were

What happened next was

My Life's Work

I am a great believer in luck.
The harder I work, the more of it I seem to have.

—COLEMAN COX

When I got serious about my career: _____

_____

_____

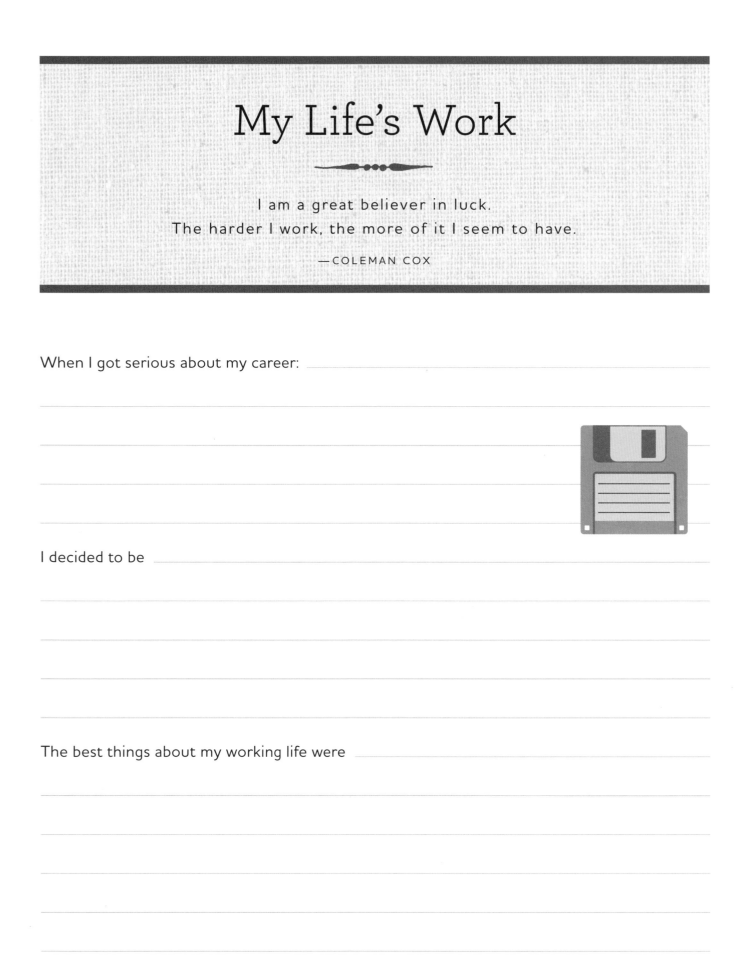

_____

I decided to be _____

_____

_____

_____

The best things about my working life were _____

_____

_____

_____

_____

What I didn't like about my work: _____

_____

_____

_____

What I did right in my career: _____

_____

_____

_____

_____

Something I would have done differently: _____

_____

_____

_____

_____

_____

What I would like to be remembered for in my working life is _____

_____

_____

_____

_____

_____

What I learned from my working life that I want to share with you: _____

_____

_____

_____

_____

Love & Marriage

No, there's nothing half so sweet in life, as love's young dream.

—THOMAS MOORE, from *Irish Melodies*

I first met your grandmother (where and when) _____

_____

_____

_____

_____

What first struck me about her was _____

_____

_____

_____

The story of how we got together: _____

_____

_____

_____

_____

We dated for (how long?) _____

_____

_____

Some of the things we did together were _____

_____

_____

I knew we were in love when _____

_____

_____

How I met her family (or my impressions when I got to know them): _____

_____

_____

_____

_____

The story of how we decided to commit to one another: _____

_____

_____

_____

_____

_____

_____

_____

Our wedding took place on (date) _____

at (location) _____

_____

Some of the people in attendance were _____

_____

_____

_____

_____

_____

_____

The thing(s) I will always remember about our wedding: _____

_____

_____

_____

Our honeymoon or first big trip after our wedding was to _____

_____

_____

When we were first married, we lived

Our days were filled with

Some of our favorite things to do back then included

We had/did not have a pet

Our best friends in those days were

Something I want to share with you about being young and in love is

Where I've Lived

It takes a heap o' livin' in a house t' make it home,
A heap o' sun an' shadder, an' ye sometimes have t' roam
Afore ye really 'preciate the things ye lef' behind.

—EDGAR GUEST, *from Home*

1. ADDRESS: _____

_____

_____

When I lived there: _____

Why I lived there: _____

_____

_____

What I remember most about this place: _____

_____

_____

2. ADDRESS: _____

_____

_____

When I lived there: _____

_____

Why I lived there: _____

_____

What I remember most about this place: _____

_____

3. ADDRESS: _____

_____

_____

When I lived there: _____

Why I lived there: _____

_____

What I remember most about this place: _____

4. ADDRESS: _____

_____

When I lived there: _____

Why I lived there: _____

_____

What I remember most about this place: _____

_____

CHAPTER FOUR

About My Child, Your Parent

Your Parent Is Born!

A baby is God's opinion that life should go on.

—CARL SANDBURG, *from Remembrance Rock*

When we were pregnant with your parent, we were living in

We earned our livings working at

,

Your parent was born on

At this location:

At this time:

The story of your parent's birth is

We brought the baby home to _____

_____

Here's why we chose your parent's name: _____

_____

_____

_____

Three words to describe your parent as a baby are _____

_____

What I remember most vividly about our first year as parents is _____

_____

_____

_____

A story that we always used to tell about your parent as a baby: _____

_____

_____

_____

Other things I want to tell you about your parent's early childhood: _____

_____

_____

_____

_____

_____

_____

Your Parent as a Child

The childhood shows the man, As morning shows the day.

—JOHN MILTON, from *PARADISE REGAINED*

As a toddler, your parent was

A story I remember from when your parent was small:

Who looked after your parent when we were not home:

As a child, your parent liked _____

_____

_____

_____

Some places we used to take your parent as a child: _____

_____

_____

_____

Your parent's first organized activities or preschool included _____

_____

_____

Your parent's sibling(s)' names and ages (your aunts and uncles): _____

_____

_____

Your parent's friends: _____

_____

_____

Some of your parent's favorite games or toys included _____

_____

_____

_____

We had a pet that _____

_____

_____

Your parent loved these stories or books: _____

_____

_____

_____

_____

_____

Some of your parent's favorite songs: _____

_____

_____

_____

_____

_____

Your parent's favorite foods: _____

_____

_____

Your parent refused to eat: _____

_____

A funny thing your parent said or did: _____

_____

_____

_____

Something your parent did that made me proud: _____

_____

_____

_____

Some of my favorite memories of your parent as a child: _____

_____

_____

_____

_____

Notable personality traits your parent had as a child: _____

_____

_____

_____

About Your Parent's Education

The love of learning, the sequestered nooks,
And all the sweet serenity of books.

—HENRY WADSWORTH LONGFELLOW, *Morituri Salutamus*

YOUR PARENT ATTENDED ELEMENTARY SCHOOL AT

Your parent got to school by

Your parent's grades were

Some of your parent's friends during these years were

After school, your parent would

Activities and sports your parent was involved in:

A memory I have of your parent from elementary school:

YOUR PARENT'S MIDDLE SCHOOL WAS

Your parent got to school by

Your parent's grades were

Some of your parent's friends during these years were

After school, your parent would

Activities and sports your parent was involved in:

A memory I have of your parent from middle school:

Your parent's high school was

Your parent got to school by

Your parent's grades were

Some of your parent's friends during these years were

After school, your parent would

Activities and sports your parent was involved in:

Overall, your parent's strongest subjects in school were

What your parent loved/didn't love about school:

About Your Parent as a Teen

——◆◆◆◆——

The young always have the same problem—how to rebel
and conform at the same time. They have now solved this by
defying their parents and copying one another.

—QUENTIN CRISP

As a teenager, your parent's interests included

I remember your parent liked to wear

Your parent's hair was

Music your parent listened to:

Books your parent liked as a teen:

Movies and television shows your parent was into:

Something your parent did as a teenager that made me proud was

 And something that got your parent got into trouble was

Your parent's strongest personality traits as a teenager were

A story I'd like to share with you about when your parent was a teenager is

About Our Family Life

If tolerance, respect, and equity permeate family life, they will translate into values that shape societies, nations, and the world.

—KOFI ANNAN

When your parent was growing up, some things we would do together as a family were

During the summer, we would

Some memorable family trips we took included

Our home life was _____

_____

As a parent, I was _____

_____

For me, some triumphs and challenges of being a parent were _____

_____

_____

_____

Our family values included _____

_____

_____

Lessons I learned as a parent that I'd like to share with you _____

_____

_____

_____

About Your Parent
as a Young Adult

—•◦•—

When I was a boy of fourteen, my father was so ignorant I could
hardly stand to have the old man around. But when I got to be
twenty-one, I was astonished at how much he had learned in seven years.

—MARK TWAIN

After high school, your parent _____

_____

_____

As a young adult, your parent's personality was _____

_____

_____

_____

The first place your parent lived independently was _____

_____

_____

_____

Your parent's first paying job was

As a young adult, your parent's relationship with me was

I was proud of your parent for

I knew your parent had truly become an adult when

Something to ask your parent about this time of life:

Your Parents

Don't please my folks too much. Don't laugh at my jokes
too much. People will say we're in love!

—OSCAR HAMMERSTEIN II, from Oklahoma

Your parents met (where and when)

The first time I met your other parent was

I knew their relationship was going to be special when

A memory I want to share with you about your parents is

About Your Birth

The best babysitters, of course, are the baby's grandparents.
You feel completely comfortable entrusting your baby to them for
long periods, which is why most grandparents flee to Florida.

—DAVE BARRY

Here's how I found out you were going to be born: _____

_____

How I felt when I learned I would be your grandparent: _____

_____

How I first met you: _____

_____

To me, you looked like _____

_____

How I used to entertain you: _____

_____

My first or favorite memories of you as a baby include _____

_____

_____

_____

CHAPTER FIVE

Family Heritage

Our Family Traditions

In our family, there was no clear line between religion and fly-fishing.

—NORMAN MACLEAN, from *A River Runs Through It*

Our family beliefs include

Our family tries to live by these values:

The holidays or occasions that have always been most special to our family have been

Our important holiday traditions include

A story from a favorite family gathering (where, when, who, and what happened):

Family tradition(s) that I hope will continue:

Our Family Recipes

Tell me what you eat, and I will tell you what you are.

—JEAN ANTHELME BRILLAT-SAVARIN

Some of our favorite family dishes include _____

_____

_____

_____

_____

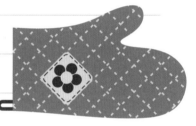

A recipe from your parent's childhood: _____

_____

Ingredients: _____

_____

_____

_____

_____

Instructions: _____

_____

_____

_____

A recipe from your parent's childhood: _____

Ingredients: _____

Instructions: _____

Family Traits I See in You

If you cannot get rid of the family skeleton, you may as well make it dance.

—GEORGE BERNARD SHAW, from *Immaturity*

Our family history includes some interesting people that I would like to tell you about:

People in our family you resemble physically include

Your personality reminds me of this relative:

Some family qualities I wish for you through your life are

Family member: _____

Trait (why): _____

Family member: _____

Trait (why): _____

Family member: _____

Trait (why): _____

Family member: _____

Trait (why): _____

CHAPTER SIX

About Life and Living

Historic Events in My Lifetime

Life is either a daring adventure or nothing.

—HELEN KELLER

Major events that occurred during my lifetime include

A world leader I admired was

A big news story that happened where I lived:

The way I've shown I care about world events is

A funny news story that I can remember happened when

A scientific breakthrough or discovery that improved my life was

A modern convenience that we didn't have when I was a child is

A part of the world that's very different now from when I was young is

Something I've learned about the world that I'd like to share with you is

My Happiest Memories

For thy sweet love remembered such wealth brings
That I scorn to change my state with kings.

—WILLIAM SHAKESPEARE, from Sonnet 29

Here are some of the memories that have meant a lot to me, which I'd like to share with you:

My happiest moments as a child:

My happiest moments as a young man:

My happiest moments in my marriage: _____

_____

My happiest moments as a parent: _____

_____

_____

_____

My happiest memory of your parent: _____

_____

_____

_____

My happiest moments with you: _____

_____

_____

My happiest moments with friends: _____

_____

_____

My happiest moment alone: _____

_____

_____

My Favorites

The great law of culture is: Let each
become all that he was created capable of being.

—THOMAS CARLYLE

My favorite places, near and far: _____

_____

_____

_____

My favorite color(s): _____

_____

My favorite food(s): _____

_____

_____

My favorite time of day: _____

_____

_____

My favorite books: _____

_____

_____

My favorite poems: _____

_____

_____

My favorite piece of music: _____

_____

_____

_____

My favorite movies: _____

_____

_____

_____

My favorite plays: _____

_____

_____

_____

My favorite works of visual art: _____

_____

_____

_____

Other things that make me happy that I hope you might like, too: _____

_____

_____

_____

_____

Me Now

Age is a question of mind over matter. If you don't mind, it don't matter.

—LEROY "SATCHEL" PAIGE

Where I live now: _____

_____

How I fill my days: _____

_____

_____

My favorite activities: _____

_____

_____

My best friends now are _____

_____

_____

What brings me joy: _____

_____

_____

_____

_____

Things that I wish I could change: _____

_____

_____

_____

_____

What I'm reading, watching, and listening to: _____

_____

_____

_____

_____

My perfect day: _____

_____

_____

_____

_____

_____

Granddad's Wisdom

We must be willing to get rid of the life we've planned,
so as to have the life that is waiting for us.

—JOSEPH CAMPBELL

If I could reach back in time and give myself one piece of advice when I was young it would be

A challenge I've faced in my life that I'd like to share with you:

How I've learned to deal with adversity:

Some things that have given me comfort in hard times:

Things to remember when you're facing a difficult challenge:

Recommended reading for good times and bad:

What my life has taught me that I want to share with you:

My Wishes for You

Beautiful dreamer, wake unto me,
Starlight and dewdrop are waiting for thee.

—STEPHEN FOSTER, from "Beautiful Dreamer"

What I hope you learn from your childhood: _____

_____

_____

_____

My hopes for your education: _____

_____

_____

_____

Some things I hope you experience in your lifetime: _____

_____

Some places I hope you will visit are

My dreams for your working life include

I hope you find a love that

I wish you a partner in life who

My greatest dreams for you:

Your Questions for Me

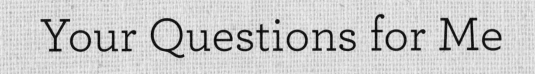

I am human, and nothing that is human is alien to me.

—PUBLIUS TERENTIUS AFER

Here is where you can ask me anything else you'd like to know about my life, and I'll do my best to answer: